The
JOHN LENNON
Collection

Cover: © 1983 Annie Leibovitz/Contact Press Images
Interior photos: Bob Gruen/Star File Photo Agency, Inc.

HAL•LEONARD™
CORPORATION
7777 W. BLUEMOUND RD. P.O. BOX 13819 MILWAUKEE, WI 53213

1970 - APOLLO THEATRE - NYC

1974 - NEW YORK CITY

1974 - ELTON JOHN & JOHN - preparing to record
"Whatever Gets You Thru The Night"

JOHN &
YOKO

1972
MADISON
SQUARE GARDEN

GIVE PEACE A CHANCE

Words and Music by JOHN LENNON
and PAUL McCARTNEY

chance _____

C'mon

1

2 Let me tell you now **3** Oh let's stick to it **4** All we are say - - *12 times*

Db

Ab7

- ing _____ is give peace a chance _____

Ab 11   Ab 13   Ab 7   Db

All   we   are

Shouts, Cheers, etc. Till fade

INSTANT KARMA

Words and Music by JOHN LENNON

POWER TO THE PEOPLE

32 bars per minute

Words and Music by JOHN LENNON

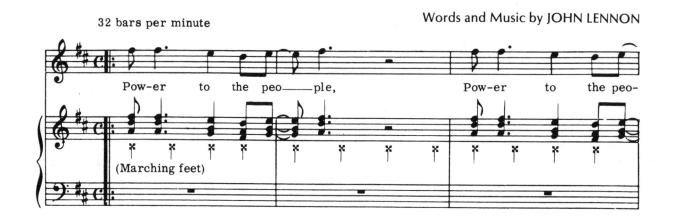

Pow-er to the peo——ple, Pow-er to the peo-

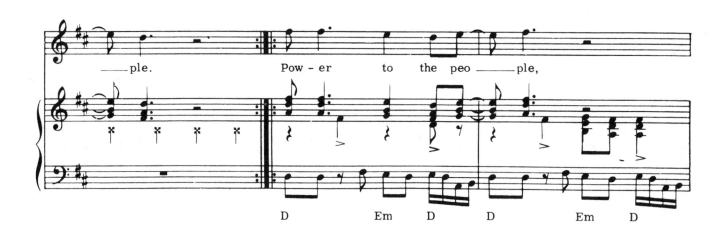

——ple. Pow-er to the peo——ple, Pow-er to the peo——ple,

D   Em   D   D   Em   D

Pow-er to the peo——ple, Pow-er to the peo-

D   Em   D   D   Em   D   D   Em   D

4th time
To Coda ⊕

——ple.   Pow-er to the peo-ple right on. ——   You
2. A mil-lion
3. I gon-na

D   Em   D   D   Cmaj7   D

say you want a rev - o-lu ————tion,   we'd bet-ter get   on   right a - way—
work - ers work —— in' for no ———— thing,   you bet-ter give them what they real - ly own
ask   you com — rades and bro———thers,   how do you treat your old wo- man back home—

Em

——   Well let's get   on   your feet, ——   end of the street,— sing-ing
——   We got - ta put you   down— when we come in - to ——— town, — sing-ing
——   She's got - ta be her - self —— so she can give us——— help, — sing-ing
              Oh well ——

12

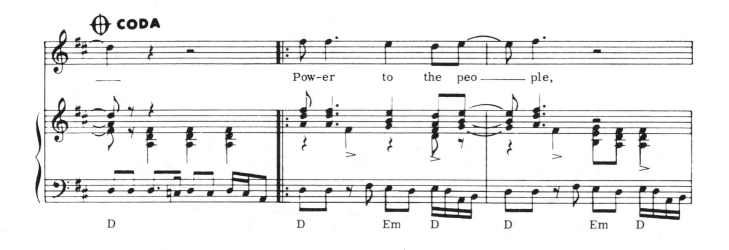

WHATEVER GETS YOU THRU THE NIGHT

Words and Music by JOHN LENNON

#9 DREAM

Words and Music by JOHN LENNON

20

LOVE

Words and Music by JOHN LENNON

Love is   real,___   real is   Love;___
                       touch is   Love;___
                       free is   Love;___

MIND GAMES

Words and Music by JOHN LENNON

25

JEALOUS GUY

Words and Music by JOHN LENNON

(JUST LIKE) STARTING OVER

Words and Music by JOHN LENNON

Moderately, with a strong beat

been   too long since we   took the time.__ No   one's   to blame. I   know time flies__   so
day   we used   to   make it, love.__   Why can't we   be   mak - in' love nice and

quick - ly!
eas - y?

But   when   I   see   you,   dar - lin',
It's   time   to   spread   our   wings   and

it's   like   we   both   are   fall - ing   in
fly. Don't   let   an - oth - er   day   go

IMAGINE

Words and Music by JOHN LENNON

40

WOMAN

Moderately slow

Words and Music by JOHN LENNON

I'M LOSING YOU

Words and Music by JOHN LENNON

1980 - JOHN & SEAN - Hit Factory

BEAUTIFUL BOY

(Darling Boy)

Words and Music by JOHN LENNON

Moderately

Close your eyes,_ go to sleep,_ say a lit-tle prayer._ The

mon-ster's gone._ He's on the run,_ and your dad-dy's here._
Ev-'ry day,_ in ev-'ry way,_ it's get-ting bet-ter and bet-ter.

DEAR YOKO

Words and Music by JOHN LENNON

WATCHING THE WHEELS

Moderately, in 2

Words and Music by JOHN LENNON

Peo - ple say I'm cra - zy
Peo - ple say I'm la - zy,
Peo - ple ask - ing ques - tions,

do - in' what I'm do - in'.
dream - in' my life a - way.
lost in con - fu - sion.

D.S. ℅ (no repeats) al Coda ⊕

Coda

I just had to____ let it go.____

I just had to____ let it go.____

1980